TIVOLI
VILLA D'ESTE

VILLA GREGORIANA - HADRIAN'S VILLA

Published and printed by

NARNI - TERNI

Photographs: SENZANONNA, SPERANDEI, BIANCHI, VESCOVO.

Text: Loretta Santini

English Translation: Brian Williams

Photolitho: S.A.R.Offset s.r.l., Rome.

© Copyright by CASA EDITRICE PLURIGRAF
S.S. Flaminia, km 90 - 05035 NARNI - TERNI - ITALIA
Tel. 0744 / 715946 - Fax 0744 / 722540 - (Italy country code: +39)
All rights reserved. No Part of this publication may be reproduced.
Printed: 1997 - PLURIGRAF S.p.A. - NARNI

INDEX

TIVOLI AND ITS SPLENDID VILLAS

Tivoli and its surrounding area is one of the most interesting of all visits in the environs of Rome, and one that is crammed with artistic treasures. It is splendidly set in what is known as the Roman Campagna - i.e. the area which was for centuries the meeting-point, and battleground, of many peoples. For as many centuries it also witnessed the progressive expansion of the splendid civilisation of Rome, which decided the fate of much of the then known world. It is an area that was loved and frequented by famous people of all eras, who embellished it with their splendid villas and impressive gardens, drawn there by its closeness to the City, by the presence of thermal waters in the Bagni di Tivoli (the "acque albule") which were especially appreciated in ancient times. It was also prized for the richness of its watercourses (it is crossed by the Aniene and the Tiber) and its roads, and especially for the beauties of the landscape.

The affection and interest aroused by the town of Tivoli among scholars, poets and students of art thus have their origins in the extraordinary richness of its artistic heritage, which is essentially concentrated in a number of fine villas, both from Roman and Renaissance times. These have also made Tivoli one of the most popular destinations of Italian and international tourism.

The exceptional artistic treasures of the Villa d'Este and Hadrian's Villa and the spectacular qualities of the surroundings of the Villa Gregoriana offer the visitor a splendid marriage between architecture and nature, and are full of new and unexpected moments of revelation.

The Aniene, the small river which crosses the territory, often takes a lead in shaping the environment; its waters and those of its tributary streams create the magnificent and imposing - and sometimes awe-inspiring - landscapes of the Villa Gregoriana, as well as the stunning water displays of the Villa d'Este and

Hadrian's villa. In the latter, the largest of all the imperial villas known to us today, it is the original character of the architecture and the beauty of the buildings which strikes us most. Down the ages, they have preserved the exceptional personality of an Emperor who was a profound connoisseur and lover of literature and classical studies. He devoted profuse energies to devising and creating a residence which was intended to respond as closely as possible to the aesthetic canons of beauty laid down by the Greek culture which he so admired.

The residence, huge in extent - in fact it occupies 300 hectares - is full of enchanting gardens and exquisitely designed buildings. Unexpected technical devices often strike us in these buildings; some of them were to be taken up as models by some of the greatest architects of the Renaissance and Baroque eras in Italy.

Hadrian's love of literature led him to commission buildings which were intended to house libraries, with collections of all the most important works of antiquity. His admiration for Greek culture, his passion for the art and the great monuments which he had witnessed on his journeys through the provinces subject to Rome, led him to create, and at times to copy in his residence, great masterpieces of architecture and sculpture.

As well as the grand scale and elegance of the buildings, the many triclinia and nymphaea and waterpools, we are also struck by the variety of the landscape and the beauty of the views which can be seen from the belvedere, also constructed by the Emperor himself.

The Villa Gregoriana, on the other hand, offers above all the superb, imposing spectacle of nature itself: dizzying precipices, astonishing natural caves, high, roaring waterfalls, remains of ancient Roman villas, unforgettable panoramas. The re-ordering of the whole area carried out in the nineteenth century for Pope Gregory XVI led to the channelling of the waters of the Aniene, and the

creation of a park of exceptional beauty and great romantic impact.

The magnificent Villa d'Este, with its garden full of fantastic stage-set compositions, with its 500 fountains and the special enchantment of its many little waterfalls and its luxuriant vegetation, offers the visitor moments of unforgettable and fascinating experience. The river Aniene, skirting the edges of Tivoli, with a number of tributary streams, has made it possible to create one of the most fantastic parks ever seen, and a villa of rare beauty.

The real begetter of this complex was Cardinal Ercole d'Este, who wanted to transform the former Benedictine monastery where the seat of the Provincial Governor had been established, into a residence which would equal the splendours of the great residences of the Roman emperors. The genius who designed this, one of the finest of all Italian gardens, was Pirro Ligorio, assisted by numerous engineers and hydraulic experts in designing and creating fountains where the play of water is often enriched by melodious sounds produced by subtle hydraulic machines.

Tivoli, then, includes in its historic centre some of the most significant monuments of the Renaissance, such as churches and palaces, and above all the villas which give so much lustre to its art and its reputation. It has become a real jewel of a city, and a place where over the centuries cultural and artistic experiences of the highest rank have met and mingled with each other.

TIVOLI

Tivoli stands in the Roman Campagna, in a pleasant, sunny position stretched along the slopes of the Ripoli and Catillo hills, both of which face out over a wide panorama and over the valley of the Aniene, the river which winds around the edges of the historical centre, and with its many waterfalls gives a very distinctive character to the area and to the city itself.

Tivoli was loved and frequented as a place of vacation and relaxation from ancient times. Witness to this can be found in the splendid villas which give the town its greatest prestige and its attraction as a tourist centre.

The name derives from the legendary Tibur - an Arcadian - who according to tradition was the founder of the city along with his brother Catillus. The same figure is found at the origin of the name Tiburtina, the title of the main arterial road linking Tivoli with Rome.

Tivoli was probably of Latin origin - some scholars have identified prehistoric villages in the surrounding countryside which can be ascribed to various races - and it attained special importance in the Roman era when, after being subjected by Furius Camillus in the 4th century BCE, it was adorned with temples and public buildings, and above all became the out-of-town residence of some of the most prestigious figures of the City, who built splendid villas there. The city was further enriched by mediaeval, Romanesque and Gothic buildings, which bear witness to the importance that Tivoli continued to have in later ages than the Roman, and in particular in the age of the Communes, when it enjoyed a long period of autonomy. From 1816 onward it was incorporated into the Papal State, and after 1870 passed to the Italian nation. A visit to the historic centre includes the Villa d'Este and the Villa Gregoriana, which because of their special character and vast size will be dealt with separately since they constitute entities in themselves.

THE HISTORIC CENTRE

Access to the town is by the Via Tiburtina, which runs directly into the centre of Tivoli. The first place met with is Piazza Garibaldi, with its orderly flower-beds and greenery, and its nearby garden with a *Monument to the fallen of two wars.* (by C.Fontana). Adjoining this is Piazza Trento, where the **Church of Santa Maria Maggiore** is to be found.

The church was first built in the fifth century, but reconstructed in Romanesque/Gothic style in the thirteenth. An arcaded portico stands in front of it, with a seventeenth century bell-tower beside it; inside, the plan is of a triple nave still containing works of some interest, such as a Cosmatesque pavement, and paintings by Torriti, Baccio di Montelupo and Bartolomeo Bulgarini; the latter being the artist of the triptych figuring the *Madonna enthroned between Saints.*

Beside the Church is the entrance to the magnificent **Villa d'Este,** which will be described separately later. In the nearby Piazza Annunziata stands the seventeenth century **Palazzo Bischi** and a former baroque church.

Via della Missione leads into the **Mediaeval Quarter;** a district with a strong character of its own. The narrow streets and ancient houses bring back the fascinating atmosphere of the past, and create picturesque corners and unexpected glimpses of the old town.

There is a particularly characteristic series of houses in Via Campitelli, among which can be seen a very old house with its outside staircase and gallery.

Behind the Villa d'Este stands the **Church of San Pietro (Chiesa della Carità)** greatly restored after the damage suffered in the bombardment of the second world war.

On Piazza del Colonnato - a name deriving from the remains of columns which can be seen on the façades of the houses - is the **Church of San Silvestro**, built in the twelfth century in Romanesque style, but later transformed. Fine frescoes adorn the interior: those in the apse are the originals from the 12th century, and portray the Legend of San Silvestro.

The Church of San Silvestro was built in the 12th century in the Romanesque style, and later transformed. It has valuable frescoes in the interior; those in the apse are the original ones from the 12th century, portraying the Legend of San Silvestro.

THE CATHEDRAL

This is the most important religious building in Tivoli. It stands on what was a sacred area in Roman times, in all likelihood the place where the temple dedicated to Hercules stood. Its present appearance, with a façade enhanced by a large portico, dates from a seventeenth century rebuilding, while the bell-tower is the original Romanesque one.

The interior, also from the seventeenth century, has a number of significant masterpieces of Italian art. One work, of great dramatic impact, is the **Deposition of Christ amid angels and saints** one of the most expressive of all wooden sculptured groups of the thirteenth century. Every figure seems isolated from the others, almost as if closed away in timeless grief and profound silence. Another magnificent work is the **Triptych of the Redeemer**, a valuable painting of the twelfth century portraying the Redeemer, surrounded by *Episodes from the New Testament*: this is framed

Interior of the Dome: Triptych of the Redeemer - the Redeemer seated on a throne in a position of blessing.
It is covered with an embossed silver coating dating from the 13th century.

by a fine panel in embossed silver, created in the mid fifteenth century. The site on which the Duomo (Cathedral) stands and the area adjacent to it were part of the ancient Roman Forum, as witness the actual remains found here. It has already been mentioned that the Cathedral stands on the site of a temple. In the area beyond it some finds have been made which can be traced to the public buildings that stood here, and in particular the so-called *mense ponderarie*, i.e. the buildings used in Roman times for the checking of weights and measures.

On the edge of the town can be seen two temples known by the names of the **Temple of Vesta** and the **Temple of the Sybil.** The names which have been bestowed on them are in fact uncertain, since they have been attributed by some scholars to the divinities Hercules and Tiburnus.

Situated in positions high on the summit of what was once the acropolis of the city, and facing on to a

Interior of the Dome: Deposition of Christ - wooden sculptured group with figures on a natural scale.

The so-called temple of Vesta, based on a circular plan, with Corinthian columns, is situated in a dominant position where the acropolis once stood.

narrow gorge and on to the park which surrounds the Villa Gregoriana, they are splendid examples of ancient sacred buildings. Their state of preservation is due to the fact that they were transformed into churches in the Christian era.

The Temple of Vesta (1st century B.C.) has a circular plan, and an elegant row of columns separated by the cella of an ambulatory.

The other sacred building (probably dating from the 2nd century B.C.) has a rectangular design.

Near the Temple of Vesta is the Temple of the Sybil, in the Ionic style, and based on a rectangular plan.

The trip around Tivoli (the Villa Gregoriana will be the subject of a separate section) ends with a visit to the **Rocca Pia.** The well-preserved fortress, proud and imposing, dominates the whole panorama of the city.

Built on the orders of Pope Pius II Piccolomini (from whom it takes its name) just after the middle of the fifteenth century, it was intended to defend the place from rebels against Papal rule. It was later extended by Pope Alexander VI Borgia, and became the favourite seat of Popes, artists and men of culture. This was where Ignatius of Loyola, the founder of the Jesuit Order, obtained the recognition of his own rule.

The Rocca is on a quadrangular plan, with the angles given added character by four powerful cylindrical, battlemented towers. The rooms inside are used for cultural events of all kinds, and of a very high level.

A visit to Tivoli may also include Piazza Santa Croce, with its fine Renaissance houses, Piazza del Municipio, Piazza Palatina, with a mediaeval portico, the sixteenth century houses along Via Palatina, and the remains of the **Roman Amphitheatre** (2nd century A.D.), the **Church of San Giovanni Evangelista** (a Renaissance building which has interesting frescoes by Antoniazzo Romano) and the sixteenth century **Palazzo Croce**, with its elegant little courtyard. There are also other buildings from the sixteenth century and a mediaeval tower-house with an elegant marble window.

We should also point out the graceful campanile of the church of **San Michele**, and the church of **San Biagio**, whose origins date back to the fourteenth century but which was later transformed. Inside there are some remains of fifteenth century paintings of the Tuscan school. Inside the church of Sant'Andrea are fine columns of cipollino marble, thought likely to be plundered material. Remains of Roman Baths and other buildings have been found on the site.

Rocca Pia and the remains of the amphitheatre.

THE VILLA D'ESTE

The Villa d'Este owes its fame to the extraordinary combination of gardens and fountains which adorn the building and make it one of the most evocative and fascinating of all architectural complexes. The aristocratic mansion itself is a brilliant example of environmental planning: the beauties of nature, trees, flowers, watercourses, co-exist wonderfully with the fantasy of the marble perspectives of the fountains and the noble, elegant character of the residence.

The idea for the Villa came from Ercole d'Este, Cardinal of Ferrara. When he was appointed Governor of Tivoli in 1550, he sought to transform the former Benedictine Convent - which was already the seat of the governor - into a magnificent villa which would emulate the country hous-

A view of the gardens of the Villa d'Este. because of its famous fountains it is a favourite tourist site for thousands of visitors.

es of ancient Rome, and above all, the splendid residence of the Emperor Hadrian.

To realise this aim, he entrusted the plans to Pirro Ligorio, an architect, a writer and a great enthusiast for antiquity, and he surrounded himself with many celebrated artists who were to join in the embellishment of his residence.

In only a few years, the aim was achieved and the villa took on the magnificent appearance which it still bears today.

On his death in 1572, it passed to the d'Este family, which continued the work of completion and enrichment. After the marriage of Beatrice d'Este to Ferdinand of Habsburg, it became the property of the Habsburg family, who held it until 1918, when it passed to the Italian state. From that time, the Villa, considered a national treasure, has been

PLAN

A Courtyard
B Fountain of Venus
C Loggia
1 Grotto of Diana
2 Fountain of the

Great Globet (Bicchierone)
3 Rometta
4 Avenue of the Hundred Fountains
5 Foutain of the Oval
6 Foutain of Bacchus

7 Fountain of the Water Organ
8 Fountain of Neptune
9 Fishpond
10 Fountain of the Dragons
11 Fountain of the Owl

and the Birds
12 Fountain of Persephone
13 Fountain of Ariadne
14 Fountain of the Mete
15 Fountain of Nature
16 Rotonda of

the Cypresses
17 Fountain of the Eagles
18 Roman Villa
19 Staircase of the Bollori
20 Avenue of the Hydrangeas

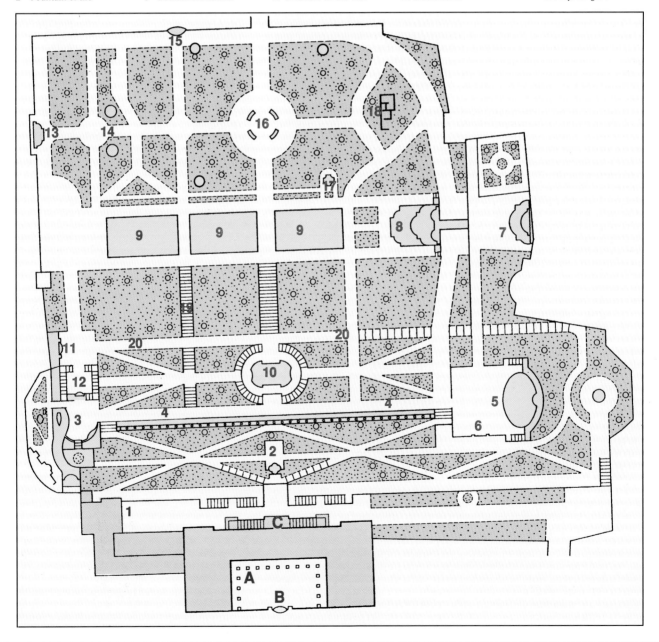

entirely restored and returned to its ancient splendour, after many years of decay due to the virtual abandonment which it had suffered.

Today it has almost completely recovered its former splendour, and presents the visitor with a combination of wonderful interiors and the extraordinary fascination of the great park. Here, immersed in the greenery of graceful flowerbeds and thick vegetation formed by centuries-old trees, are fine fountains alternating with chattering waterfalls, all of them set in remarkable architectural surroundings.

The villa is entered from Piazza Santa Maria Maggiore, beside the church of the same dedication, on to which one wing of the courtyard backs. In the past, this was the secondary entrance to the mansion: the main one was on the opposite side, at the end of the route followed by the ancient Via Tiburtina.

An elegant fifteenth century portal with a rounded marble arch formed the entrance to the Villa. The coat-of-arms which can be seen above it comes from the old Governor's Palace, and belonged to Cardinal Caravajal, who was a former governor of Tivoli.

A frescoed **corridor** with B*iblical subjects* leads into the **Courtyard (A).** This is arcaded on three sides, while on the fourth, flanking the church, it was transformed by the architect Pirro Ligorio, who made use for the most part of the ancient structures of the cloister of the monastery.

On the side of the Church of Santa Maria Maggiore can be seen the so-called **Fountain of the Sleeping Venus (B);** the goddess appears lying above an ancient sarcophagus resting on a bath: this, in turn, is framed in an architectural perspective with double columns sustaining a rounded arch.

The courtyard of the Villa - the Arcade and the figure of the Sleeping Venus can be seen.

Fountain of the Sleeping Venus - detail.

UPPER APARTMENT OR OLD APARTMENT

This was the original nucleus of the residential quarters of Ippolito d'Este, Cardinal of Ferrara and Governor of Tivoli. It is made up of ten rooms, completely covered in frescos (the main artist was Livio Agresti, a sixteenth century painter), and with period furniture, valuable decorative objects and paintings. The rooms are arranged around the throne room, and look out over the Garden of the Villa d'Este.

* The Great Hall or Throne Room: a splendid room with a ceiling decorated with grotesques and with frescoes portraying *The Aniene* and the *Temple of Vesta*. On the walls is a copy of a portrait of *Pope Julius* II by Raphael, and works by Perin del Vega and the school of Andrea del Sarto.

* The Library: decorated with some reproductions of paintings by famous artists, this was once the study of the Cardinal.

* The Bedroom: the most important work here is the splendid wooden ceiling carved by Bolingier. It includes the coat of arms of the Este family, showing an E*agle in the Garden of the Hesperides*. On the walls are paintings by Correggio and Daniele da Volterra.

* Rooms 4 and 5: are decorated with friezes and contain paintings by the Caracci brothers and Barocci,

* The Chapel: on the altar is the so-called *Madonna di Reggio*, painted by Agresti, alongside which are painted *Scenes from the life of Mary*, and figures of the Sybils and prophets. The decoration of the room is completed by some stuccos of the 18th century. The antechapel was restored in the first years of the present century.

* Rooms 6,7,8,9,10: a fine collection of paintings can be seen on the walls of these rooms.

LOWER OR NOBLE APARTMENTS

The group of rooms round the central salon were the official reception rooms of the Governor.

Central Hall (Room 1). This room is sumptuously decorated with frescoes, sculptures and mosaics. The ceiling was painted by Girolamo Muziano, and completed by Federico Zuccari. The fresco, framed in a perspective stage-setting of columns, deals with the subject of the B*anquet of the Gods*, and in the corners are portraits of *Appollo, Bacchus, Diana and Ceres*. On one wall there is also a fountain built out of mosaic and plaster and containing a reproduction of the Temple of Vesta, and the symbol of the Este family, showing an E*agle plundering the apples of the Garden of the Hesperides*.

On the opposite wall to the one with the fountain there is a *View of the Villa*. The painting has historical and documentary value since it shows the earliest plan of the villa.

Rooms to the right of the Central Hall: there are five rooms, decorated with *Mythological Scenes* and *Episodes connected with the history of Tivoli*.

* Room 2: *Catillus, General of the Fleet of Evandros, landing in the Lazio; the brothers of Catillus; the response to the riddles; the construction of the walls of the city; the struggle against the neighbouring peoples; the choice of the name Tibur* (Livio Agresti).

Lower Apartment - The Central Hall.

Above: *Lower Apartment - the great fresco on the ceiling of the Central Hall, portraying the Banquet of the Gods.*

Right: *Lower Apartment - Room 3, Stories of King Anius: the King dies in the Aniene while he is chasing his daughter's kidnapper.*

* Room 3: *Stories from the past of Tivoli: The Tiber, The Aniene and the sources of the city; Phoebus' chariot* (on the ceiling); *Stories of King Anius and Inone* (the young girl who was to be transformed into the Sybil of Tivoli).
* Rooms 4,5 & 6: these are frescoed with *Stories of Noah and Moses*, and with a number of Views.
Rooms to the left of the Central Hall (in the space between the two groups of rooms there is a **loggia (C)**, facing out on to a splendid view of the park, and connected to it by a double-ramp staircase, an elegant architectural device by Ligorio);
*Rooms 7,8,9 & 10: the decoration of all these rooms is sumptuous. We should mention in particular the fresco in Room 7 figuring the *Council of the Gods*, and the *Labours of Hercules*, a work by pupils of Muziano and Karcher. In the next room - known as the Room of the Philosophers - there are paintings of the *Allegories of the Virtues, the Sciences and the Arts*, and busts of ancient philosophers.

Lower Apartment - Room 2: Catillus landing on the shores of Latium (Livio Agresti).
Lower Apartment - Room 7: The Chariot of Phoebus (Livio Agresti).

Lower Apartment - Room 7: Portrayal of the Spring Albula - detail.

Upper Apartment - Portrait of Cardinal Marcello Santacroce (V.Manenti, 1600-1674).

THE GARDENS

Passage between the house and the garden which lies in front of it is obtained by means of the elegant double staircase which descends from the loggia mentioned above. It opens in scenographic fashion on to the main avenue which comes close to the villa and then branches out into a series of paths skirting the flower beds and criss-crossing the whole park.

On the right of the main avenue stands an elegantly designed pavilion; this is the so-called "panoramic loggia", known as such because an amazing view over the surrounding countryside can be had from it. As we have mentioned, the splendid garden of the Villa d'Este is what confers fame and lustre on the Villa itself; it is certainly one of the finest of all examples of the Italian Park.

The green area is harmoniously divided up into a complex array of beds rich in flowers and trees, many of them centuries old. The flowerbeds themselves are bounded by shady walks, forming a very effective geometrical pattern. Along the paths are low stone walls, often covered in moss and delicate maidenhair fern. In the midst of all this ebullient greenery can be found marble sculptures, low walls and seats. And perhaps the greatest point of interest is that everywhere there are little streamlets, tinkling fountains and small and large cascades tumbling noisily down. The designer of this fantastic environmental architecture has succeeded in harnessing the waters of the Aniene and other minor watercourses to create a wonderful stage-setting of water-jets (there are more than 500 in all) which give the garden the image of a place which is spectacular and yet tranquil at the same time.

A work of genius and fantasy, at once refreshing and restful. The mannerist taste which is characteristic of the park and the many fountains gives the whole place a vast fascination, and it has been the model for many of the Italian gardens which were to adorn the great houses of the nobility from that time onward.

Pirro Ligorio can thus be considered the inventor of a perfect and intriguing symbiosis between architecture and nature. No small contribution was made to this by the other engineers and experts whose genius went into creating, for each fountain, high-precision mechanisms such as in the case of the Water Organ, that of the Owl and the Birds, or the Dragons, and that of the Mete. Each of these, thanks to skilful and studied channelling of the water, succeeded in producing sounds or movements of the water, which today, unfortunately, can no longer be seen and heard.

It can be stated with certainty that the Villa d'Este represents an absolute masterpiece of environmental architecture, and also of hydraulic engineering, and it is this together with its extraordinary beauty that has made it famous all over the world.

The rear façade of
the Villa d'Este,
the loggia and the
double ramp
staircase which
leads down to the
Garden.

A VISIT TO THE GARDENS

THE GROTTO OF DIANA (1)

This is reached along a small path which leaves the villa, running at a lower level.

The creative fantasy of the designers (Curzio Maccarone and the Calandrino brothers) here devised a hollow and a fountain richly ornamented with mosaics, enamels and stuccos. In the floor-pavement there are also figurines, varied scenes and ornamental designs of different types. On the walls are *mythological scenes* in stucco which was once gilded. The many statues which adorned the grotto were representations of the pagan deities, among them Diana herself, the Amazons and Minerva. Most of them have now been removed to Roman museums in order to conserve them better.

Diana's Grotto, although to a great extent despoiled of its works of art, and although it has lost the richness of some of its decorations (many were covered in gilding), nevertheless remains one of the richest and most precious possessions of the Park.

THE FOUNTAIN OF THE GREAT GOBLET ("BICCHIERONE") (2)

This was not created until nearly a century after the building of the Villa. Some critics attribute its design to Bernini, an artist who worked for a long time on the improvement of the residential complex.

The gracious and elegant fountain has a base in the form of a shell, and above this rises a great chalice-shaped cup, which was what gave rise to the name of the "biccherone" or "Great Goblet".

Above: *The Grotto of Diana.*
Below: *Detail of the Fountain of the Great Goblet.*

Rometta (3)

The name of this fountain - which means "Little Rome" - provides the key to understanding the elements which make up its construction. The statues in fact represent some of the characteristic features of the City; the River T*iber* and the A*niene*; R*ome* (which is the large figure seated at the centre of the fountain) and the *she-wolf suckling the twins*. The *boat* with the *obelisk* symbolises the Tiber Island, but also Papal Rome. The design of the fountain and the style of the sculptural groups has pointed to the hand of Gian Lorenzo Bernini, who certainly worked for a long time on improvements to the Villa.

THE AVENUE OF A HUNDRED FOUNTAINS (4)

A theatrical succession of fountains and waterspouts follows the whole length of the path which crosses the garden, and connects the Rometta with the Fountain of the Oval. The thick vegetation, the extraordinary play of the light and shade, the perfect symbiosis of nature and architecture, the rhythmic succession of the water outlets and the constant trickling of the water itself create a unique and fantastic atmosphere. The sculptures decorating this fountain are particularly fine: they include *animals*, *obelisks* and floral decorations. Many of them have been damaged by the passage of time, but their beauty nevertheless remains intact. Almost nothing, however, remains of the bas-reliefs which once portrayed *scenes from the Metamorphoses of Ovid*.

THE FOUNTAIN OF THE OVAL (5)

The effect created by the complex of small waterfalls and the play of the water which flows over from the great oval basin - hence the name - and which then descends through an elegant architectural perspective broken up by niches and statues, is quite astonishing. At the top end of the constructions there is a balustrade with thin marble columns which marks the edge of a terrace. Beside it can be seen a rocky formation covered with vegetation. In the basin where the waters gather there is a large shell. The front of the parapet is decorated with ceramics.

The overall effect, which manages to produce an unexpected balance out of a variegated series of elements, is one of the most significant achievements of the designer of the villa, Pirro Ligorio.

In this fountain the waters of the Aniene were originally gathered together, and then redistributed round the rest of the garden. The sculptures which can be seen were mostly carved by Giovan Battista Della Porta, on the basis of designs by Ligorio himself. The *allegorical portraits* are by Giovanni Malenca. The statue which stands at the peak of the highest part, representing a winged Pegasus, is particularly striking.

Beside the Foutain of the Oval is the **Fountain of Bacchus (6).**

THE FOUNTAIN OF THE WATER ORGAN (7)

Its fame is linked not only to its beauty and the imposing nature of its construction , but above all to the hydraulic organ which at one time could be brought into play by the waters. It was a brilliant and inspiring mechanism, created by Claudio Vernard, by means of which, through the simple mechanical action of the water which ran through appropriately designed tubes, aerial sounds were brought into play, and these produced notes not unlike those from the pipes of an organ.

The fountain, planned by Pirro Ligorio, is baroque in design. The construction rises above a basin : the perspective is based on four huge thalamons including two lateral niches (with statues of *Orpheus* and *Apollo*), and one central one. In this is set a kiosk (an inspired addition by Bernini), within which the hydraulic organ itself is located. The decoration of the whole complex is full of ornamental motifs, in which bas-reliefs alternate with mythological figures and architectural elements.

The upper part of the complex is finished off by two great volutes and a huge eagle standing above the coat of arms of Cardinal Alessandro.

Above: *The Fountain of the Water Organ.*
Below and on the right-hand page: *The Fountain of Neptune.*

THE FOUNTAIN OF NEPTUNE (8)

This theatrical and magnificent fountain has the task of linking the Water Organ with the fishpond at a lower depth.

It is of more recent origin, and was designed by Attilio Rossi, who partially incorporated the previously existing nymphaeum designed by Ligorio.

The phantasmagorical interplay of the water-jets, the power and foaming rage of the waterfall, and the harmonious interweaving of the multiple sponts of water, all creates a striking impression, as the water plunges from one basin to another.

The statue of Neptune which was part of the original project by Ligorio, presides over the lowest basin of the fountain.

View of the Fishpond from the Fountain of Neptune.

THE FOUNTAIN OF THE DRAGONS, OR THE FOUNTAIN OF THE WIND MACHINE (10).

The fountain is situated on the Avenue of the Hydrangeas (20). Its own form and the complex system of connections between the paths and gardens around it, make it outstanding in conception and harmonious in the interplay of its different parts. Particular note should be taken of the interweaving of the stairways which have the architectural function of linking the different levels of the fountain.

Its name derives from the carved group of dragons which dominate the center of the basin. At one time it was also known as the **Fountain of the Wind Machine** because it was equipped with a mechanism (designed by Tommaso da Siena) which moved the waters in such a way as to simulate sounds, cracks and claps which followed one another in impressive fashion.

The fountain in its entirety is the work of Pirro Ligorio, who sought to create a stage-like architectural complex, with the aim of making this the absolute centre of the whole garden.

The fountain is made up of a great elliptical basin, set among the linking stairways. At the centre is the sculptural group representing the *dragons* - monsters with gaping mouths, carved with alarming realism. The inspiration for these came from the coat of arms of Pope Gregory XIII, who paid a visit to the Villa. It is said that on this occasion, to render suitable homage to the Pontiff, Ligorio carved the group in the course of a single day (1572). The Fountain of the Dragons was once adorned with statues and decorated, in the bed of the basin, with paintings figuring mythological scenes.

A long staircase known as the **Scala dei Bollori (19)** links the Avenue of the Hundred Fountains to the Fishpond. About half way down the staircase, it is crossed by the evocative **Avenue of the Hydrangeas (20)**, which runs parallel to the fishpond and the Avenue of the Hundred Fountains.

The Scala dei Bollori.
The Avenue of the Hydrangeas.

THE FOUNTAIN OF THE OWL AND THE BIRDS (11)

Its fame and name are linked to the birdsong which used to emerge from subtle and complicated hydraulic mechanisms present inside the fountain. The melodious sounds seemed to come from the bronze statuettes of the animals which once adorned the complex. Once again the Villa d'Este amazes us by the exceptional originality of its effects, and the care taken in searching for theatrical settings, as well as by the ingenuity shown by the many technicians and artists in finding devices of astonishing effect.

The Fountain of the Owl and the Birds, for instance, apart from producing animal sounds, was designed in such a way that the animals could suddenly appear and disappear among the bronze branches which had been created and beautified in the building of the fountain. It is quite easy to imagine how these effects, now virtually all disappeared, would have won the enthusiastic admiration of those who lived in the villa and those who visited it.

Even though many of the decorations which once adorned the fountain are vanished, there remains the image of an elegant and sumptuous architectural design, the central part of which is imposed on a great arcade flanked by two columns. At the centre of the main arch a waterfall descends, scattering its waters in the basin below. In the upper part of the complex appears the coat of arms of the Este family.

THE FOUNTAIN OF PERSEPHONE (12)

Four columns mark out a nymphaeum flanked by niches. The ensemble, baroque in character, is harmonious and elegant, and has the function of linking the surrounding area to the Fountain of the Dragons.

THE FOUNTAIN OF ARIADNE (13)

This fountain is simple and linear, in fact almost geometrical in form, and although it has been despoiled of its statues and ornaments, it nevertheless adds grace to the garden by its form and elegance.

The Fountain of Ariadne rests against the perimeter wall of the garden in the stretch where it opens on to a wide and characteristic view of the Roman campagna.

FOUNTAIN OF THE METE OR THE SWEATING COLUMNS (14)

It takes its name from the representation of the *Sweating Statue*, one of the most famous of Rome, characterised by the slow descent of drops of water resembling gouts of sweat.

The Fountain of the Owl and the Birds.

The Fountain of
the Sweating
Mete.

THE FOUNTAIN OF NATURE (15)

This is found on the edge of the garden, near the former entrance to the villa. It takes its name from the statue portraying *Mother Nature* in the semblance of Diana of the Ephesians (the sculptor was Giglio della Vellita). The goddess, framed in a rocky cave in the form of an arch, is represented - according to traditional iconography - as many-breasted, and from each breast drops the milk which constitutes the symbol of fertility.

THE ROTONDA OF THE CYPRESSES (16)

This is a very effective haven of greenery, placed symmetrically in the garden with the Dragon Fountain in such a position that its view embraces a large part of the garden and provides glimpses of many of the fountains. It is a silent green oasis: the lengthy shadows of the cypresses create a fairy-tale atmosphere of calm.

THE FOUNTAIN OF THE EAGLES (17)

This stands near the Fishpond and its elegant architecture fits perfectly into the greenery of the flowerbeds and the park.

In the garden of the Villa d'Este, hidden among the trees, there are remains of a **Roman Villa (18).**

On the left and on the opposite page: *The Rotonda of the Cypresses.*
Below: *The Fountain of the Eagles.*
On pages 40-41: *play of the water in the Fountain of the Oval.*

THE VILLA GREGORIANA

The Villa Gregoriana, another of the fascinating gems of Tivoli, stands at the edge of the city, where the Aniene, skirting the fringes of the residential area, widens into a broad curve and then plunges into a deep gorge.

The landscape - truly exceptional and breathtaking - is characterised by rocky escarpments, steep cliffs, paths which are barely marked, and rocks protruding from the slopes of Mount Catillo. The waterfalls formed by the descent of the Aniene plunge noisily down, emphasising the exceptional character of this landscape and adding to its fascination. Dark tunnels and passages open between the cliffs and among the trees, offering the visitor constant surprises and new visions.

The beauty and exceptional character of the natural surroundings is enhanced by the variety of the most startling viewpoints, the incredible richness of the vegetation, and the constant variety of the stones which protrude from the ground; by the remarkable steepness of the gorge and the magnificence of the views. The constant sound of the water of the Aniene which falls to the bottom of the gorge in the Grand Cascade, raising clouds of minute pulverised droplets, evokes deep sentiments in the viewer.

The same strong impression is made by the Grotto of the Sirens, and the Grotto of Neptune: these hollows show clear signs of the erosion caused by time. The waters have carved out the rocks; at times they have formed stalactites and stalagmites, and here they still rule unchallenged, with their waterfalls and their relentless, bustling activity.

In the midst of all this beauty, and of so much natural activity, the work of humanity is even more enhanced. Among the greenery there appear the grandiose remains of the Roman villa of Vopiscus, and on the ancient acropolis there is the elegance of the temple of Vesta, with the circle of its fine Corinthian columns.

The Villa Gregoriana was conceived as a grandiose garden which would include and enclose the splendid natural landscape of Monte Catillo and the river Aniene. The work was mostly carried out in the thirties of the 19th century, at the behest of

Pope Gregory XVI, from whom the villa takes its name. Among other things the planning of the area involved the digging of small tunnels and channels which were aimed at regularising the flow of the river's waters, which had on many occasions overflowed their banks and flooded the territory around, causing substantial damage. The work of diverting the streams, carried out by the architect Clemente Folchi, achieved the aim of stabilising the flow of the water by giving definite shape to the course of the river, the waterfalls and hence of the land itself.

The Villa Gregoriana is reached across the **Ponte Gregoriano**, a large-scale construction built by order of Pope Gregory between 1831 and 1846. It was almost completely destroyed by the bombardment suffered during the last war, but subsequently rebuilt as an exact copy of the 19th century original.

The bridge consists of a single great arch, resting on pylons. It has a characteristic geometric decoration, with alternating black and white blocks. The arms of Pope Gregory XVI adorn it.

A visit to the Villa Gregoriana, as we have suggested, involves a long and fascinating journey amid the inspiring natural beauties of its landscape. The tourist is helpfully guided by notices which point out the most suitable routes to follow.

A stairway, descending the cliffs, leads first to the Temple of Vesta (see tour of the city of Tivoli), and then to the **Grand Cascade.** The spectacle is amazing. The waters, descending dizzily between green-covered walls for a drop of over 120 metres (390 feet) then gather in the gorge below and send up clouds of fine spray.

The volume of the waterfall has declined considerably since the last century because the strength of its waters has been harnessed by the power stations which lie further up the course of the Aniene, for the production of electricity.

The Grand Cascade has always attracted crowds of tourists for many centuries because of its exceptional beauty; numerous tributes witness to this popularity, left by people

who have wished to inscribe their names on the stones in the Galleria Gregoriana.

The itinerary takes the visitor on to the **Horse-shoe**, a small belvedere which looks out over the waterfall itself.

It then goes on to the lower part of the Waterfall, and enters the Gorge of the Aniene by way of tunnels. Here the Cascatelle come into view, i.e. the lesser branches of the main waterfall. The path then leads first to the **Cave of the Sirens** and then to the **Cave of Neptune**. Both are natural hollows created by the timeless work of the water. The scene which they offer is unforgettable; the cascades fall vigorously, creating special and memorable effects among themselves. The deafening roar which accompanies the fall of the Aniene adds to the effect of the place, and renders it even more impressive.

Colours too play a basic role in the scene: the fantastic irridescence of the little pools and the reflections of the waters on the stalagtites and stalagmites held to stress the uniqueness of the place.

Within the bounds of the Villa Gregoriana stand the ruins of the **Villa of Vopiscus**: these visible ruins bear witness to the greatness and the beauty of the Roman buildings which even in ancient times were praised by poets and writers.

Other remains of the Roman era have come to light during the digging of tunnels and galleries: these have included burial sites, stones, part of the ancient acqueduct, and structures belonging to Ponte Valerio.

The *Temple of Vesta and of the Sybil* stands at the edge of the Villa Gregoriana, and is mentioned in the guided tour round the historic city. These buildings provide a fitting completion to this remarkable portrait of the past.

A visit to the Villa Gregoriana, as we have suggested, involves a long and fascinating journey amid the inspiring natural beauties of its landscape. The tourist is helpfully guided by notices which point out the most suitable routes to follow.

THE SURROUNDINGS OF TIVOLI

An interesting and pleasant tour around the fringes of Tivoli takes one from the Ponte Gregoriano to the Belvedere over the grand Cascade, and to the Cascatelle, the lesser falls, and then on to the remains of the *Villa of Quintilius Varus* (2nd century C.E.) a Roman building of substantial proportions.

In the surrounding countryside, other archaeological remains can be found, dating from the age of the Temples (*Temple of Mundus and of Hercules Victor*), and especially those of the **Sanctuary of Hercules Victor**. This was built in the 1st century B.C.E. alongside the Via Tiburtina. It was rectangular in design, and it is given an imposing air by the substructures which support the archaeological area where among other finds, remains of a theatre and other public buildings have come to light.

Another itinerary which is historically and archaeologically interesting is the one which follows the Via Tiburtina, and after passing the turning for Villa Adriana, continues on in the direction of Rome. At the point at which it crosses the Aniene, there is the **Ponte Lucano**, built in travertine; this was the scene of important historical events. In fact, considered a strategic point for communications with the City, it was a campsite for the armies of Frederick I Barbarossa, Pope Hadrian IV (12th century), Giovanni Colonna (13th century) and the Orsini (15th century).

In the surrounding countryside one can find the **Sepulchre of Plautius**, a Roman monument of the 1st century C.E., but re-used and transformed in the Middle Ages. Its shape recalls that of the tomb of Cecilia Metella on the Appia in Rome.

After passing **Villalba**, famous for the travertine quarries which furnished so much material for the villas of Tivoli, wwe reach **Bagni di Tivoli**, a town which is famed for its hot springs. These are the celebrated *acque albule*, once much appreciated, and sought after ever since ancient times; their virtues have been sung by many writers. They are used for therapeutic baths in the establishment which has been built on the spot.

A short way from the town, the *Solfatura* is worth a visit; this is also known as the *Queen's Lake*. This smooth stretch of water, also greatly appreciated in the Roman era, as witness the remains of baths and temples near at hand, is intensely and strikingly coloured, because of the chemical elements in the water.

51

HADRIAN'S VILLA - THE VILLA ADRIANA

The enormous complex of the Villa Adriana is one of the most important of all ancient Roman monuments, and above all one of the most fascinating. The vastness of the central building, together with the subsidiary palaces, the baths, triclinia, theatres, splendid nymphaea and great pools of water; the storehouses and accommodation for guests, and the libraries, all go to make this the greatest of all known imperial residences. We only have to realise that the whole complex occupied an area greater than 300 hectares and was thus a good deal larger than Nero's Domus Aurea, his splendid and grandiose residence in Rome. We could really describe it as a mini-city rather than a villa, so complex was the variety of buildings which composed it.

An ideal city, where everything was functional, where everything was to exalt harmony and beauty, and where everything was combined to recreate the ideals of the classical age.

The residence, built on the outskirts of Tivoli - it is reached after turning off the Via Tiburtina, and is about two miles outside the city - is one of the favourite and best-loved tourist attractions of the place, along with the beauties of the city itself. The fullness of its historical memories and the splendid artistic remains make this one of the jewels of antiquity. The villa's name derives from that of the Emperor Publius Helius Hadrianus (76 to 138 C.E.), the successor of Trajan. he ruled from 117 to 138 C.E. He was an enlightened ruler; rather than dedicating himself to further terri-

torial expansion, he made it his concern to amalgamate and coordinate the vast empire. He moved from one province to another, supervised the local administration, and awaited the building of major works, not least the famous Vallum Hadriani, or Hadrian's Wall, which marked the furthest boundaries of the Roman Empire in the extreme north of Britain.

An intelligent, cultured sovereign, and a lover of art, in the course of his numerous journeys he gleaned much experience from the contact with different civilisations. He studied the most interesting monuments with great care, absorbing the part which interested him most in each of them. He had a particular love of Greek culture, from which he derived his own philosophical musings, and his artistic notions. From Greek monuments - but also from Egyptian ones - he drew the inspiration for the planning of the buildings in his villa. The sculptures which adorned his residence were mostly copies of the statues carved by the greatest Greek artists.

He strove to transmute these experiences in the construction of his own residence, of which it is believed he himself was the designer. The villa was thus made to measure for his own sensibilities, the knowledge he had acquired, the dreams which he wished to realise. It was an ideal city, where everything was functional, where everything was meant to be a hymn of praise to harmony and beauty, and where everything combined to recreate classical ideals.

A restless and visionary spirit, reflective and curious, he was able to convert his profound sensibility into the planning of the building complex and the architectural ideas used. And above all he gave it an innovative impulse which was to be taken as a model by architects and sculptors who lived centuries after he did. Hadrian's Villa was built in the early years of the 2nd century of the Christian Era; specifically between 118 and 134, as can be seen from the inscriptions found on bricks and marbles and as is confirmed by scholars of the period.

The Emperor only lived in his longed-for residence for a short time, as he died at Baia in 138 C.E.

For many years the villa remained unaltered; the rulers who followed Hadrian only made use of it in the summer period. Soon it was

PLAN

1 Plastic model of the Villa
2 The Pecile
3 Room with the exedrae or Apsidal Room
4 The "Cento Camarelle"
5 Lesser Baths
6 Greater Baths
7 Vestibule
8 The Canopus
9 The Museum of the Canopus
10 The Academy
11 Temple of Apollo
12 Olive Grove and Tower of Roccabruna

THE IMPERIAL PALACE & THE THREE PERISTYLES

13 Nymphaeum of the Palace
14 Arcaded Court with the Fishpond
15 Praetorium
16 Barracks of the Palace Guard
17 Summer Triclinium
18 Room of the Doric Columns
19 Nymphaeum
20 Piazza d'Oro (A)
21 Peristyle of the Palace (B)
22 Private Library
23 Cryptoportico
24 The Bath-house with the Heliocaminus
25 Room with the Apse or Room of the Philosophers
26 Island Villa or Maritime Theatre
27 Third Peristyle or Courtyard of the Libraries
28 Latin Library
29 Greek Library
30 Hospitalia
31 Room with three naves
32 Imperial triclinium
33 Pavilion of Tempe - Terrace of Tempe - Valley of Tempe
34 Small Temple of Venus
35 Greek Theatre
36 Palestra

stripped of its most precious marbles, its finest statues and all the materials which were used for the construction of other buildings in Tivoli. The emperors Caracalla and Constantine also despoiled it, both of them anxious to embellish their own palaces with the masterpieces from Hadrian's residence.

Works such as the *Discobulus* by Myron, one of the most celebrated of all artworks of ancient Greece, and the statue of *Antinous*, Hadrian's lover, ended up in various museums in the capital. The same fate met the statues of Praxiteles, the celebrated Greek sculptor; the portraits of fauns and telamons and animals, the tragic masks, the stunning mosaics like those portraying *Doves and Centaurs*, belonging to what came to be known as the "Little Palace". The friezes which decorated the baths and the libraries, too, everything has been transferred over the centuries to Rome (Capitoline Museum, Vatican Museum, National Museum), and to Naples (the Archaeological Museum). Some treasures have even found their way abroad.

As far back as 1461 the humanist Pope Pius II Piccolomini noted bitterly the sad state of neglect of the villa. Ippolito d'Este, the Maecenas of the Villa d'Este, caused the first studies to be made on the site by his architect Pirro Ligorio.

Pope Alexander VI Borgia, at the end of the 15th century, displeased like his predecessor at the grave deterioration of the villa, charged that what remained of the complex should be brought back to light. This work was continued by Alessandro Farnese and Cardinal Carafa, and went on almost uninterruptedly throughout the following centuries.

Final restoration was decreed by the Italian state after it acquired the site from the Braschi family (relations of Pius VI) who had in the meantime become its proprietors. The work of excavation and study still continues today, and aims to bring the whole complex back to light, to give back as much integrity as can be restored to its ancient beauty and grandeur.

An intelligent and erudite sovereign, a lover of the arts; in the course of his many journeys he absorbed the various experiences and contacts with different civilisations.
He had a special love for Greek culture, from which he derived his own philosophical musings and his conceptions of art.
He attempted to transmute these experiences in the construction of his dwelling, of which he himself seems to have been the designer.

A VISIT TO HADRIAN'S VILLA

A visit to the villa can be divided up into three sections. The first of these is made up of the central part of the complex, which one reaches immediately after the entrance, and which includes the Pecile and the adjoining buildings. After this we move on to the southern side, where the Canopus is situated, and much further out on the edge, the olive grove, the tower of Roccabruna and the Academy.

The second sector includes the heart of the Villa itself, with the majestic buildings of the imperial palace, the three peristyles and all the numerous buildings which are linked to it. It also includes, after moving further out to the periphery, the Valley of Tempe and the Pavilion of Tempe.

The third section includes all the northern area and reaches the Palestra, the small circular temple, and the Greek theatre.

THE PLASTIC MODEL OF THE VILLA (1)

This is found in the Entrance area. It makes it possible to view an ideal reconstruction of the villa, and recognise the whereabouts of the various buildings. It also makes it clear immediately how vast the complex was, and how integrated and daring its design. By looking first at this reconstruction of the villa it will also be easier to get a sense of direction from the remains of the citadel, and choose the route which seems most appropriate. The numbers shown on the chart will help the visitor to take account of the position of the buildings, and choose which sector to visit at any given moment.

THE PECILE (2)

This forms the entrance to the villa, and is made up of a huge arcade extended around four sides (232 x 97 metres). Outside it appears like an imposing stone wall, the height of which (although in fact lower than the original, which was probably 12 metres tall) today still reaches 9 metres (27 feet). One of the sides has a double arcade covered with a tiled roof. The internal space is occupied by a large fishpond (106 by 26 metres). Some scholars have surmised that there was once a riding track here; in the past it used also to have gardens. This area, which could make use of both light and shade, was intended for the walks that the Romans loved to undertake after a heavy meal, in order to refresh the spirit and enjoy conversation. It opened over a wide view of the Roman campagna. The Pecile is a typically ancient Greek construction: the one which has survived in Athens, which is a good deal smaller, had its outside walls painted. The origin of the word *poikile*, forerunner of pecile, which meant a painted surface, confirms this custom.

pages 58-59: *The large pool of the Pecile.*
Below: *The plastic reconstruction of the villa, which can be found near the entrance.*

The imposing outer wall of the Pecile.

THE THRONE ROOM, OR APSIDAL ROOM (3)

This stands alongside the Pecile, in its south-eastern corner, and its special feature is the exedrae which give variety to the construction, bestowing a trilobial plan. This is one of the many novel architectural notions which Hadrian himself dreamed up, and it is also one of the forms which most greatly interested the Renaissance and Baroque architects. The western side of the Pecile rests on a large substructure (a massive containment wall), which reaches all the way to the Baths, and then heads for the southern section of the Villa. Above this substructure, a number of rooms have been built, all aligned longitudinally; they have been dubbed the **Cento Camarelle (4).** They may have been the storerooms or the dwellings of the servants. Access to these rooms was provided by external staircases, which ended in pensile galleries.

The Apsidal Room is one of the many novel architectural experiments introduced by Hadrian.

The Lesser Baths (5)

So-called to distinguish them from the Greater Baths, from which they are separated by a Courtyard or Vestibule, they can be recognised by their traditional division into *frigidarium* (an eliptic-shaped room with bathtubs in the big lateral apses; the *calidarium* (a large round room) and the *tepidarium*.

The octagonal room with the perimeter wall with its straight lines and convexes in alternation was probably the *podyterium*, used as a changing room.

This building, possibly reserved for women, is of small dimensions and has some very innovative architectural features: for example, the octagonal room, where the search for an original way to give variety to the walls by the alternation of straight and curving lines, and the roofing of the room with a large dome over ten metres in diameter, show the creativity of the architect.

Several rooms intended for physical exercise or for relaxation and conversation flank the traditional bathrooms.

The decoration of the place consisted of murals, mosaics and sculptural groups.

The Lesser Baths.

THE GREATER BATHS (6)

The building, complex and original in some ways in its architectural design, attracts the attention by the clever way in which the parts are articulated and by the imposing dimensions of the structure. It was reserved for men.

Provided with the classical areas of the warm water baths (*calidarium, tepidarium, frigidarium, laconicum or sauna*) it is divided up into a series of lesser rooms, mostly reserved for services, but also for relaxation and casual meeting.

The largest room - the *frigidarium* - is at the centre of the complex. It has a large apse, and this was once covered with a superb cross-valuted roof, now partly collapsed. The two big basins, one semi-circular in shape (the one set into the wall of the apse) and the other rectangular, were originally adorned with columns.

The decoration of some of the rooms is particularly interesting. Paintings, sculptures, mosaics and stuccos alternate. The stuccos present in the vault of the room next to the largest one are particularly striking.

In some rooms, hydraulic systems can be seen, used for heating or cooling the water. A clever system of damp-coursing and canalisation which passed through pavements and walls distributed hot vapours which were produced by boilers.

Near the bath buildings is a large space which was used as a **Palestra**, where gymnastic exercises were performed. In the *spheristerium*, on the other hand, hand-ball games were played.

The care of the body was of immense importance to the Romans. They not only looked after their physical health through exercises and cold, warm and hot baths, but also cared for the mind. The Baths in fact were a place of relaxation and at the same time an opportunity to meet, to discuss politics and literature, business or fun. They thus provided a means of binding together social life and strengthening human relations.

The Greater Baths.

THE VESTIBULE (7)

The building situated near the Lesser and Greater Baths is known as the Vestibulum, but its actual purpose is not by any means clear. Some say that it was a linking structure, while others have advanced the theory that it was in fact one of the entrances to the Villa.

The Vestibule, some of the remains of which are still to be excavated, is made up of an arcaded courtyard punctuated by exedrae and niches, and surrounded by various rooms, the purpose of which is not known.

THE CANOPUS (8)

The justly famed Canopus is fascinating because of the extraordinary and skilful blend between nature and architecture, the exceptional originality of its design, and the remarkable atmosphere which the reflection of the elegant columns and delicate sculptures creates in the great "mirror" of still water. The beauty of the valley in which it is sited adds to the fascination of the Canopus, as do the limpid qualities of the water and above all, the historical memory of the places visited and loved by the Emperor Hadrian himself.

Canopus was in fact a small Egyptian city which grew up near Alexandria, close to the Nile Delta. It was built by the Spartans who chose this name because they wished to commemorate the prefect of the fleet of Menelaus. The town, as the historian Strabo records, stood in the middle of a green valley watered by a canal derived from the Nile, and near the Sanctuary of Serapis, one of the best-loved and most visited shrines of antiquity.

Hadrian wished to reproduce this pattern, and above all to recreate the atmosphere of what he had seen and admired in Egypt - he probably also wanted to commemorate and pay homage to Antinous, his young lover, who had met his death in the waters of that place, possibly by suicide. For this purpose he had a small valley dug out, and here the great pool was placed - the so called Nilotic Channel - which in his mind must have recalled the course of the river Euripus.

The pool is rectangular and measures 119 by 18 metres. Along the more extended sides there were marble steps - now vanished - and here stood the pavilions used for various services, or as places to welcome guests.

The northern side of the pool is marked out by an **exedra**, in other words a very elegant circle of Corinthian columns surmounted alternately by architraves and arches. The statues which can be seen today are copies of the originals, preserved in the local Museum. They represent *Mars, Mercury and Minerva*.

The banks of the canal are adorned

on one side by a series of columns and on the other by large *caryatids and Sileni*, statues measuring more than 2 metres in height. The caryatids are inspired, in size and design, by those which adorned the Erechtheum on the Acropolis in Athens.

At the end of the canal, on the southern side, there is the most imposing and theatrical building of the Canopus, i.e. what remains of the Temple believed to have been dedicated to Serapis (a tradition which cannot be confirmed says that it was built in memory of Antinous). The colonnade is in fact a **Nymphaeum**, formed by a large niche flanked by smaller niches, and crowned with a dome divided into sections and decorated with mosaics. Previously, jets of water issued from the Nymphaeum, creating an extraordinary fountain.

The Nymphaeum was flanked by other smaller ones, and by various buildings used for services and for accommodation. One of the rooms was a large **triclinium** , apparently intended to accommodate banquets in summer time.

We possess a description of Egyptian Canopus by the Latin writer Strabo: from this account we can deduce that Hadrian's reconstruction was carried out with a good deal of free adaption.

The Canopus,
deservedly
famous, owes its
enchantment to
the extraordinary
and skilful blend
of nature and
architecture, and
the exceptional
originality of the
complex.
The atmosphere
provoked by the
reflection of the
elegant columns
and delicate
statuary in the
still pool of water
adds yet further to
the magic.

THE MUSEUM OF THE CANOPUS (9)

The building houses architectural materials, sculptural groups and everything else that has been found during the excavations at Hadrian's Villa.

In order to preserve the image and the atmosphere of the great residence, plaster copies of the statues have very often been placed in the archaeological site itself, and the originals transferred to the Museum, in order to afford them adequate protection.

Many of the finds have been substantially restored and reconstructed in the various rooms with the aim of making some of the architectural elements easier to understand - for example, some of the roofs which originally covered the buildings.

Several groups of sculpture are of special interest; they include:

* *The Amazon of Phidias*: a magnificent copy of the statue by Phidias, one of the most famous in Greek art;

* 4 *caryatids and* 2 *Sileni*: these once stood along one side of the Pool of the Canopus. The caryatids are similar to those which decorated the Erechtheum on the Acropolis of Athens.

* *Mars, Mercury and Minerva*: these are copies of Greek originals: they were placed in the Exedra of the Canopus, and are partly mutilated.

* *Venus of Knidos*: a reproduction of the famous statue by Praxiteles, carved in the 4th century BCE.

* *Caracalla*: a bust of the Emperor.

* *The Crocodile*: a fine sculpture which stood alongside the pool of the Canopus on the side opposite the Caryatids.

* *Busts of famous figures*;

* *Tibur and Nile*: these are the symbolic figures of the rivers. The Tiber represents Rome, and thus the heart of the Empire; the Nile is perhaps the river that Hadrian loved best, and which he reproduced in miniature in the Canopus.

* *Statues of athletes*;

* *Satyr*

The Museum also houses various architectural fragments and decorative elements, including columns, capitals, friezes, vases (those decorated with vegetable motifs being especially fine), fragments of furnishings, mosaic tesserae, stuccos and pieces of fresco.

THE ACADEMY (10)

The name is applied to a series of imposing buildings sited in the midst of the greenery in a splendid panoramic position.

Some of the decorations recovered from one of these buildings are of special note.

In one of the rooms, with an octagonal plan, the characteristic motif of the buildings of Hadrian's villa can be found: the alternation of linear and convex strips on the walls, which was to be such an inspiration to the artists of the Renaissance and Baroque eras.

Another fine building is the round one known as the **Temple of Apollo (11)**: in reality this is a two-floor room with a small dome. Some scholars have advanced the theory that in this sector of the villa the so-called **Little Palace** was sited - i.e. the emperor's more modest private residence. This seems to be confirmed by the extent and beauty of the works found here, such as the priceless mosaic now in the Capitoline Museum in Rome, figuring *Animals and Centaurs*.

THE OLIVE GROVE AND TOWER OF ROCCABRUNA (12)

The large area which bears this title is eight-sided and is reached by a stairway. The part above the dome was possibly a belvedere, which looked out over the Roman countryside. There is a pleasant view over the ranks of olive-trees, among them a huge one which traditionally bears the name *Albero Bello*.

THE ODEON

This is the small theatre intended for musical performances and dance. The building is quite small (its widest span is not more than 45 metres) and is well preserved. The architecture is skilfully balanced between the different parts of the theatre.

The visit to the Villa Adriana now continues to the central sector, which extends from the Pecile over a wide area towards the east, and includes a series of structures used for various purposes in addition to the actual royal residence.

THE IMPERIAL PALACE AND THE THREE PERISTYLES

This was probably the official residence of the Emperor Hadrian, and thus the ideal centre of the whole Villa. The size of the buildings and the way in which the structures are connected provides a grandiose image of the palace, even though the residential quarters have only been partly excavated.The Imperial Palace in fact included a variety of buildings and rooms, and covered an area of 50,000 square metres. The complex is designed around three magnificent **Peristyles**, which also form the heart of the villa itself. The first is the Piazza d'Oro, the Second the Peristilio del Palazzo and the third the Cortile delle Biblioteche.

The visit begins from the Pecile, and heads towards the south-eastern corner, outside the area of the peristyles.

THE NYMPHAEUM OF THE PALACE (13)

Little remains of the Nymphaeum, which had two pools, other than the large niche which provided access to the place. It stands at the base of the Quadriportico. The theory has been put forward by some scholars that there was once a stadium here.

THE ARCADED COURT WITH THE FISHPOND (14)

"Quadriportico" is the name given to the big arcade which marked off an open panoramic area partly occupied by a pool where it was possible to go fishing. The construction rests on an embankment. Within the area of the Imperial Palace, but situated near the Canopus, is the **Praetorium (15)**, a massive building characterised by a series of big arcades. This was possibly used as a warehouse, and as the barracks of the Praetorian Guard, which Augustus had instituted as the Emperor's personal defence corps.

PAGES 72-73: *The Quadriporto (Arcaded Court) with the Fishpond.*
Below: *The Imperial palace - the Nymphaeum.*

THE BARRACKS OF THE PALACE GUARD (16)

This was the building used to house the Guard. The barracks has two storeys, and the rooms are arranged around a big central hall.

THE SUMMER TRICLINIUM (17)

The dining room used during the summer period. An exedra adorned with niches has survived from this structure.

THE ROOM OF THE DORIC COLUMNS (18)

This is one of the most beautiful and elegant of the palace rooms. It is rectangular in shape; along the perimeter there is a row of slim fluted columns which support a splendid barrel-vaulted roof. The room was taller than the arcade, and was lit by windows let into the wall above it.
Scholars have assumed that justice was administered in this building.

THE NYMPHAEUM (19)

This small graceful building, not unlike others of the type found in the Villa, occupied an area between two of the peristyles of the Imperial Palace - the Piazza d'Oro and the Paristilio del Palazzo.

Left: *The room with the Doric Columns.* Following page and above: *The Summer Triclinium with tower; the Greek Library.*
Below: *The Barracks of the Guard.*

A) The first of the Peristyles is known as the **Piazza d'Oro (Golden Place) (20)** because of the splendour of its decorations and the sumptuous and refined arrangement of the various elements. The area is defined by double arcades, adorned in the upper section with 60 columns. Various rooms form a sort of crown, including an octagonal one, possibly the Imperial Hall, and a vestibule, which is also octagonal. These two places, in the unusual formation of the walls, where curved and straight sections alternate, show an exceptional skill in finding completely original architectural forms.

(B) THE PERISTYLE OF THE PALACE (21)

This was a wide arcaded space, the columns of which were built in brick, judging by what has been disinterred and reconstructed.

THE PRIVATE LIBRARY (22)

This was made up of niches intended to hold the cases and shelves for the books.

THE CRYPTOPORTICO (23)

This is a partially buried arcade linking part of the Palace to the third Peristyle, or Courtyard of the Libraries. The vault still has some of its mosaic decoration.

THE BATH-HOUSE WITH THE HELIOCAMINUS (24)

The building still possesses its arcaded *frigidarium*, complete with swimming pool, and it has a circular room intended for hot baths: the hot air was supplied through an ingenious system which united the heated air from the furnaces coming from the steam courses in the walls, with the sun's heat (conveyed by the *heliocaminus*). This seems to be confirmed by the five enormous windows which are let into the walls.

APSIDAL ROOM, OR ROOM OF THE PHILOSOPHERS (25)

It is so-called because the niches in the room probably housed busts of ancient philosophers, or of the "Seven Sages". The theory of some scholars that the main seat of the Library was here seems somewhat unlikely.

THE ISLAND VILLA OR MARITIME THEATRE (26)

This is an enchanting place, and a small architectural masterpiece. It is theatrical and imaginative in design, and at the same time completely harmonious throughout.

The building is on a small scale, but artfully structured, and elegant. It has a circular plan, with a fine ring-shaped arcade which creates a vestibule, resting on Ionic columns. At the centre is a canal and a pool, also circular, and not very large, and in the centre of this there is a gracious little islet, with a diameter of only 24 metres (75 feet). On the island stands a small villa which gives the name to the island; it was built as a Roman domus, but reduced in proportions so as to seem to be a miniature. Two bridges (they were originally wooden swing bridges) give access to the island.

Some scholars, because of the originality and theatricality of the little complex, have suggested that it was

The Baths, with the heliocaminus.

a theatre on the water, but there is nothing to confirm this theory. Nor does it seem credible to identify this little building with a votive chapel dedicated to the emperor, nor even the idea that links it with the Pantheon in Rome because of some analogies between their measurements. In all probability it was a place dedicated simply to rest, tranquillity and meditation.

Right and below: *The Villa of the Islet or Maritime Theatre.*

C) THIRD PERISTYLE, OR COURTYARD OF THE LIBRARIES (27)

In this area, measuring 65 by 52 metres, there are two identical buildings, considered traditionally to have been the home of the **Latin Library (28)** and the **Greek Library (29)**. Destined to contain all the most distinguished works of antiquity, they are the most visible witness to the great love of the Emperor Hadrian for scholarship and culture.

THE HOSPITALIA (30)

These were the bedrooms (cubicles) for guests of the Palace. Five on each side, they gave on to a central room which had the purpose of linking all the others. Each had at least three beds and the floors were decorated with fine mosaics.

THE ROOM WITH THREE NAVES (31)

This too had niches, and it is divided into three sections.

We now move on to the buildings of the north-eastern section of Hadrian's Villa.

THE IMPERIAL TRICLINIUM (32)

The Cortinthian capitals which surmount the columns here are notable for their elegance.

THE PAVILION OF TEMPE
- THE TERRACE OF TEMPE
- THE VALLEY OF TEMPE (33)

The Valley of Tempe was designed by the Emperor Hadrian himself, to recall the most beautiful valley of the same name in Thessaly, celebrated by the Greek Poets. He wished above all to recreate its atmosphere and perpetuate its memory by means of an ideal reconstruction.
In the area, he built a Pavilion, i.e. a building on several floors from which one could enjoy a panorama of the whole countryside, immersed in silence, and with the water flowing below, in the ditch of the Acqua Ferrata.

One of the mosaics which decorate the floors in the rooms of the Hospitalia.

It is an enchanting place, even though it has lost much of the view which once made it famous.

THE SMALL TEMPLE OF VENUS (34)

From this sacred building comes the statue of the *Venus of Knidos* preserved in the Museum of the Villa Adriana. It is a temple of exquisite elegance, with a round plan, variegated by two exedrae. The Doric columns which once marked out the perimeter have only been partly restored.

The rediscovery of this building and its identification came about as a result of a patient labour of excavation; in fact, before work was carried out on the site, it was believed that only a Nymphaeum had existed here.

One of the Exedrae is partly occupied by the **Casino Fede**, an eighteenth century building used for the administration of the archaeological site.

THE GREEK THEATRE (35)

Its modest proportions (the diameter is only 36 metres) in no way diminish the elegant beauty of the building. The surviving parts - the cavea and the proscenium area, witness to the harmonious architecture of the whole theatre.

THE PALESTRA (36)

Very little remains of this, but it is clearly discernible that the area was used for gymnastic exercise.

Above: *the Hospitalia.*
Below: *the temple of Venus.*